preludes & fugues

POETRY BY THE SAME AUTHOR

Dimensions. Victoria: Morriss, 1967.
Passages. Vancouver: Intermedia, 1975.
Liturgies. Victoria: Sono Nis, 1975.
Foraging. Vancouver: Intermedia, 1979.
Poems: New and Selected. Fredericton: Fiddlehead 1984.
Chinese Chamber Music. Vancouver: Cacanadadada, 1989.

OTHER BOOKS

Editions

Stanley Cooperman. *Greco's Last Book*. Vancouver: Intermedia, 1980.
Pat Lowther. *Final Instructions*. Vancouver: Orca Sound, 1980.
New: West Coast–72 Contemporary Poets of British Columbia. Vancouver: Intermedia, 1977.
New: West Coast Fiction. Vancouver: Pulp Press, 1984.
New: West Coast Composers. Burnaby: Simon Fraser University, *West Coast Review Books*, 1986.
Journal: *West Coast Review: A Quarterly Magazine of the Arts*. Vols. 1–21 (1966–1986). Founder & Editor.

Academic Books

Robert Heath, *Clarastella* (1650). Gainsville: Scholars' Facsimilies & Reprints, 1970.
Perspectives on Epic. Co-edited with William Strange. Boston: Allyn & Bacon, 1965.
The Voices of Prose. Co-edited with William Stafford. New York: McGraw-Hill, 1966.
Perspectives on Style. Boston: Allyn & Bacon, 1968.

preludes
& fugues

poems by

fred candelaria

CACANADADADA

preludes & fugues
Copyright © 1992 Fred Candelaria

Published by

CACANADADADA PRESS LTD.
3350 West 21st Avenue
Vancouver, B.C. Canada
V6S 1G7

Set in Baskerville 11 pt on 13½
Typesetting: The Typeworks, Vancouver, B.C.
Printing: Hignell Printing, Winnipeg, Manitoba
Cover Design: Cecilia Jang
Cover Art: Reproduction of J.S. Bach's manuscript of "Chorale Prelude: Wer Nur Den Lieben Gott Lässt Walten"

The publisher wishes to thank the Canada Council for its generous financial assistance.

Canadian Cataloguing in Publication Data

Candelaria, Frederick, 1929–
  Preludes & fugues

  Poems.
  ISBN 0-921870-19-1
  I. Title.
PS8505.A53P7 1992   C811'.54   C92-091469-1
PR9199.3.C35P7 1992

for

yee-wah

ACKNOWLEDGEMENTS

Fred Candelaria's poems have appeared in the following reviews: *Alphabet, The Anglo-Welsh Review, Antigonish Review, Canadian Forum, Canadian Poetry, College English, CV 2, Dalhousie Review, Edge, English Journal, Event, Fiddlehead, The Greensboro Review, Jeopardy, Jewish Dialogue, The Malahat Review, New Quarterly, Northwest Review, Poetry Australia, Poetry Canada Poésie, The Prairie Schooner, Prism international, Quarry, Queen's Quarterly, St. Andrew's Review, Sou'Wester, Talon, The Tamarack Review, Tish, Tri-Quarterly, Wascana Review,* and *West Coast Review.*

His poems have been anthologized in bill bissett's *end of the world speshul anthology*, Fred Candelaria's *New: West Coast–72 Contemporary British Columbia Poets*, Gary Geddes's *Vancouver: Soul of a City*, Douglas Lochhead and Raymond Souster's *Made in Canada: New Poems of the Seventies*, Florence McNeil's *Here is a Poem*, P.K. Page's *To Say the Least: Canadian Poets from A to Z*, Robin Skelton and Charles Lillard's "The West Coast Renaissance," (a special issue of *The Malahat Review*), Virgil Teodorescu and Petronela Negosanu's *Intelegind Zapada: Antologie a poetilor canadieni de limba engleza*, Morris Wolfe's *Aurora: New Canadian Writing–1979*, and J. Michael Yates's *Contemporary Poetry of British Columbia*.

The author is deeply grateful to the editors who have published his work and to the readers whose support made these publications possible.

CONTENTS

prologue

a time ago . . .

            not long since—
just a grandfather
or a grandmother away—
we once made ourselves
immortal
simply by adding names
of births and deaths
to chronicle our present
and tie it to our past
in details written
on the flyleaf of eternity
our records in the family
bible

the different scripts
themselves declared the tales
of many hands
some of them had held us
touched us   sometimes lightly
always profoundly   and forever
leaving their encoded lives
in lines of fading ink
and in our blood-flow
where their heartbeats
stilled
echo   steady in our pulse
and in our dreams

I

sea sketches

while earthworms serpent their ways
through woodwork & walls   mountains & masonry
to lair larger than snakes in caves   .
overlooking waters

waiting & watching past scaled eyes
to taste with tongues forking
the fuming air of worlds below
cliffs ground down by time & rushing currents

grinding through granite   streams crash
ever over rocks in earth-devouring rivers
into the always tides of sea's serpent waves
coiling tight around the end of land

•

seas wall in earthworks
waves well up to stalk
land's dark sand where time
drowns in the broken hour glass
over day's dull rattle
to unsettle with broken teeth
the night's slow breath

while the siren sings
astride the black octopus
her hair streaming in the salt force
and wiles her way into the sailor's nightmare

and behind her glowing
naked phosphorescence
go all shining monsters
to shark sea horses gentle
& angel fish turning
above timeless kelp beds
in green & blue visible
& invisibly burning brine

•

drowned boats hold   cling
     hang at chasm's edge
     near crumbling ledges of canyons undersea
     ocean-covered mountain ranges
     fierce in their strangeness
          no climbers there
here blind fish   deaf plants   & the unnameable
float full of grace up sheer rock face
of another world's erupting monuments
angry in inaudible titanic roars
silent sea surges falling again fathoms down

               •

steadfast anchors too will rust
     after salt covered sea creatures
     ceaseless corrosion starts

what was securely held
     drifts   wanders   breaks apart

even flotsam & jetsam   detritus of tragedy or folly
     finally sink

               •

amorphous jelly
ghosting
among amphorahs

drowned greeks
phoenicians
romans

•

beating against
the boat's glass bottom

knocking to be hauled in
after drifting ages

neither old skulls
nor skeletons

but bubbles full
of dead air

past voices saying their last
before suddenly or slowly—

tearing tears from eyes
salt melting meeting salt

•

visions & mad maps
paper schemed
& plotted in skies
among guiding stars
misguided

•

the sea is inside us
and unfathomable

deep dives are
always into the inner sea

where the mind's eye
is worthlessly blind

sighted only
by the heart's compass

•

nights
fill with absence

fogs
catch plankton's lights

shimmering offshore
on dying beaches

rotting echoes
of foghorns

serenade
the moon's blank virtue

•

breathless   silent   the sea sleeps

dreaming of mountains & rock rivers
flashing trout streams & crystal pools

all   always   moving down

flowing steadily away from freshness
returning   back to the old age of salt

•

light

blue light lifts black glass & glows through the window
three worlds submerge   emerge   merge & float together
separate   but made one by mind's dimensions

where sky & clouds crack apart under sun's fierce force
the surface roars as waves rip time from undersea sands
to smash against the boat's glass bottom

and sing the blue-white-glass-black-sky-sea-&-boat
of morning's breaking night's dark shell into dawn
shining stark on snow of foam's wave-crests

. . . before invisible silence
washes over the burning water
drowning brightness far down deep
past the endless horizon's haze

lost at sea

the sailboat
without a helmsman
drifts

with each changing tide
& wind

II

in the name of . . .

birth   and then
death   and the need
to fill the emptiness between
—a trinity to count on—then

comes desire's weather
constant in unpredictable steadiness
of storms that burn or freeze or drown
in time's dust   lust's dry rivers   & seas of fire

or a season of scents
coloured song of flowers
sight of invisible winds bending trees
slight blades of grass
—all to pass   or come again
into the endless space
between the time to be born
& the time to die

diary

however freezing
dead bolted in ice
spring breaks doors open

with soft cloudbursts of bright
(slightly beginning) to green us

●

the sun through shutters
(to resist is to be real)
shadows shape light

water waves & weaves through nets
as moon lights webs of cloud

●

one blinding blast
outlasts summer's sun-blazed breeze
so blossoms fail her sight

glowing cold freezes those eyes
into shadows   eclipse past thaw

●

stone's silenced fire
moves and rocks desert air
to mirage music   water   love

where only our rattlesnakes live
edened in venomed dream

sunday

an almost silence
but for a sky
full of crows

the prized
japanese maple
dawns

red gold
a delicate song
of the earth

autumn waves

summer dies slowly
    winds down

flowers turn inward
    withdraw
promising to bloom
perhaps
    next spring

autumn waves
    wash over
the broken
        willow branch

october

suddenly
rain fell

as we knew it would
but freezing

to turn us all inside
ourselves

it came
just this side of ice

and we
whispered into snow

a thanksgiving

to celebrate this harvest time
the white magnolia's
last five buds bloomed
in cool moonlight
leaving their fragile scent
to night's memory
sent as fit tribute
a gift to fading beauty

winter solstice

one lightning bolt makes midnight darker
(black . . . blacker . . . blackest . . .

and always the clock ticks & chimes
(fast . . . faster . . . fastest . . .

dawn was yesterday   and icy noon passed
(his sunrise glowed into blank nothing

•

but then she came at sunset
(black . . . blacker . . . blackest . . .

dense her midnight hair
and more intense

for the blaze of one white thread
burning there

snow

...and then the snow came
a blinding brightness of white
fell deep & dense
to cover paths & roads
that once led home or away
no trace of yesterday

a dog ran wild
across the dead purity
and then voices woke the air
as footsteps stirred again
in their wake
and again   the birds

bluejay

this dark bluejay sits on top the fog
flicks his tail in mid-winter
while snow still rules
and breath steams the air

the hemlock he rests on may wonder
what brought a bird there too early
for worms below the frozen ground
why is he here this time of the year

when it's yet all over   still snow-covered

is it hope   false expectation   instinct
perhaps a twitch of nerves   a synapse
before collapse into another season
of blood's illusions

crowsong

he's back
all in black
crow or raven
he's back

before robin
or sparrow
cracking the break
between snow & rain

he's back
all in black
crow or raven
he's back again

harsh song
raking the sky
with dark
circus cry

he's back
all in black
crow or raven
always back

III

william carlos williams

opened a shoe store
in paterson, new jersey
& called it the variable foot

he sold some horseshoes for pegasus
a few wingèd sandals for mercury & friends
but mostly commonsense shoes for ordinary people

impromptu

(she goes shopping with baudelaire)

shoes wear out   or whims dictate
fashionably latest choices
among sensible   comfortable styles
or designs made more to catch
the eye of the beholder
than please the foot   but what if . . .

the inspired salesman blind to descriptions
deaf to her desires deftly felt the shapely foot
decided the delicate arch's curve
should be stressed to the breaking point
and sharply pointed her toes

stopping to paint pink toenails with blood
first   of course   removing sheer stockings
down smooth thighs over round knees
around warm curves of golden calves
to the very soul of the palm sunday
of her foot about to be crucified

by high heeled mortal sins
veering close to damnation
with every step a real purgatory
redeemed only by drops of burning perfume
on the instep of her sensual foot
in the fleet dancing flash & beauty
—her divine comedy in poetics & prosody

autopsy

death's poem is life
music lived in cells
of syllables measured
foot by faltering footfall
bright pirouettes
blind stumbles & lines missed

structuring fictitious facts
real fictions
infinite shapes
graceful   grotesque   meaningless
in solid metaphysically
black & white   ink & paper

artifice

what replaces art?

armour   arrogance
masks behind masks

what replaces blood?

wine   tomato juice
coloured   perjured water

empty shoes   synthetic yarns
& stammering echoes

on æsthetic distance

1.   Beholding beauty bare,
he exclaimed, "Masterpiece!"
saying much about himself,
but little about her.

2.   The louder he proclaimed,
the more suspicious we became.
"He doth protest too much,"
we silently explained.

3.   He played everything   *ffff*
and she, *pppp*.
Everyone heard something
at first
—then nothing
at last.

4.   Anyone seen
too close up
may as well have been
too far away.

5.   When all is superlative,
nothing else can be
worth more,
and some may be
worthless.

6.   As he writes
"Doubtless,"
undoubtedly,
he doubts.

flores para los muertos

if these flowers flourish
it will be a major miracle

they've never bloomed before
dead oracles of spring

they're made of paper
to perish in recycling

or perch in illusion's
branches on the still mantle

shunned by real birds and bees

IV

the eclipse is slipping

out of the sky toward dawn
& while he waits for sleep
he dreams he is bent down
by the weight of bits
of slim light glimmering
on the wet emerald lawn
into the shape of her body's
green outline still pressed
fresh into yesterday's grass
almost as new as his taste
for tomorrow's bright dew

cleopatra in the denver airport

a woman mellow brown
in a girl's body of dark rum
mixed with yellow candlelight
wearing her ebony hair
in innumerable serpentine braids
each asp clasped by a golden clip
like her ancient egyptian crown
above black brows & darker lashes
framing her sculptured forehead
stands at the white plastic counter

perfect   ripe & demanding (as if for antony)
firm & commandingly youthful (as if for cæsar)
ruling over timeless reverie (as if for me)

catullus

that crack of his back
tells time better than clocks

her lips command eternity
(ah   too grand a notion   perhaps . . .

but can you find a better way
to demand day die than by kisses . . .

da mi basia mille

desperate   doomed   deprived   depraved
catullus needed to count thousands

had you but kissed him only once
that would have been more than he could crave

ashes

old letters make new fires burn brighter
recalling passions stored for years
earning daily disinterest in interminable
deposits of desire & vows disavowed

the roof of memory's warehouse leaks
but these lines entangle without mercy
and may not be cut but by a blow-by-blow torch

chronology

too many a sunset—
or sunrise for that matter
—no   not a honeymoon
more like vinegar than rain

neither he nor she starred
before or after dawn
night-blind they did not
see better by daylight

burned out by noon
like the morning's toast
they napped afternoons away
—until their last goodnight

the market

ladies & gentlemen

look as much as you like
but don't touch
and don't smudge
even the edge of her image

ladies & gentlemen

she walks a precipice
stalked by beasts—
priestess & sacrifice
of erotic feasts

ladies & gentlemen

what do you bid
for forbidden pleasures
hidden & treasured
deep in your id

•

attacked by svelte velvet violence
her body lives its own life sliding
and gliding down the red runway
the take-off ramp on which romp
ravishing dervishes dancing away
the illusions of perverse desires

now she steps off her altar a skeptic
antiseptic and sinless she exults

in destroying dreams of passion
with a cynical laugh's cold stare
that turns stars to frozen dust
and the perfumed air to stale
smells of her human all too human
sweat beneath her sweet hauteur

•

the nubile nubian blacker than black
& more naked than nude
from waist to crest

lewdly paints her thick nipples
a scarlet more red
than the fire of her lips

as she snakes her hips
down the silent carpet
to model whispers

& bare all her black soul
wearing nothing but sandals
& rings round each scarlet-tipped toe

her white smile
masks a panther's snarl
as she rakes the blood on her nails

in a mock caress
across every face
that lusts for her ass

•

I am a real fiction
a fact of your imagination
your work of art

a still-life in motion

a doll whose emotions are frozen
your mannequin
of plastic flesh bone & blood

like all the statues in your mind

I am your image of the virgin
or merry magdalene depraved
before—alas—she was saved

you never hear anything I say

I am as cold as the hard cash
it takes to buy the trash
I wear for you

& so long as you pay I swear

I'll be the mannequin
your eyes may always undress
the exquisite artifact you embrace

•

her sex sells as she swivels her hips
and buyers lick their lips

she's the priestess of extravagance
her elegance their profit

salomé danced with all her wiles
and herod bought her (he thought)

for the price of the prophet's head
—but all he got was her seventh veil

•

her subtle calculated sneer curved
high above hardly disguised leers
the architecture of poisoned cheer

the less near & more arch she is
the more harshly the barb
of desire pricks & tears

through veneers of fashion
& delusions of sophistication
to the basic salt of rape and tears

•

mind? why should I mind as I wind my way
down this carpeted dialogue seducing you to think
scales weigh in your favour when you buy what I wear

mind? it's not mind but my decorated body
balancing as profit in books of sales you think you see—
so kindly buy your wares unaware—really—of me

•

I'm not a used model   I'm brand new
& blessed among women because
I'm one of the few   quite tall slim & bright
enough to know my lightning looks
when too familiar will burn out   turning me
invisible   a ghost long before my beauty fades

yes   I'm a clothes-horse in this rodeo
working harder than any real cowboy
and each jaded walk down that red runway
pays & pays & pays & pays more
than he'd earn in days of roundups

if & when I want   then I'll marry
play sheba to my solomon
and though we may not
live happily *ever* after
we'll have days & nights enough
to sing our song of songs
before the next or final act

abused?   not bloody likely
amused?   yes   absolutely

    envoi
I have my own agenda and though
I may flower in another's garden
I am wholly me   stem   leaves   & bloom
so pack-up your trivial gloom
or ship out with your clichés of doom

V

theseus

ariadne amazed him

styx and stones

he writhes
in her phlegethon's black fire
until lethe releases him

20/20

brightest waking
in darkest sleep

dreaming
to see more deeply
than eyes
blindly open

étude

mandarin fingers
stroke high cheekbones

almond eyes sagely
see through ages

voice flowers
into lean music

in time lifting
and falling
to the drift
of plum petals
floating

since & until
tears wet
the sunset

buddhist nun

none but buddha
will ever
know your beauty

VI

for george berkeley

if once upon a time it was
never is there silence anymore
sounds are everywhere
as ever they may have been
even in voids between planets
where cosmic dust grinds
echoes into bone's hard static
heard in sleep's stillness absolute
resounding with absurdities
of impossible abstractions
infinities beyond imagining
where going more deeply
the more we hear beyond sound
with refined awareness,
our ears define music & chaos
harmonizing melodies of pulse
with rhythms of breath
& percussions of blood
defying death's alleged silence
until all clocks die & stop
all sound in that vacuum
of timeless perfection:
empty eternity . . .

carpe diem

bug in the mattress
no bed without at least one

biting into dreams
with teeth of doubt—
tomorrow?

itch in the night and
scratch out yesterday

a little lost blood
but don't shout
about that today

echoes from the range

what are you shooting at
ghosts inside your head
or just objective fact

the target

an act that asks for skill
of you against yourself
wind / distance / elevation / squeeze

or is it

for a kill
inside the blood
a hate beyond the pulse

hunt

willing prey are uninteresting
like flaccid fish that won't fight

it's hard tracking to find subtle signs
of wary quarry without spooking them

by giving yourself away
—never *give* yourself away

•

trapper time best catches by surprise
the hunted over horizons prospecting still
but snares snap shutting off the light
mostly the caught are old too or ill
to flee   escape   fight
and most die twitching
at wishes beyond the hill

express lane

after but one block of fast black asphalt
the clean street is cluttered with signs & signals

some seem to stay green   but most range
the various shades of yellow   jaundiced & sick

quickly to add up to odd reds   harshly blatant
as the jammed   damned lights won't change

rooftop soliloquy

slippery rungs   up the wet ladder
the one way to the roof
to look for   find   and fix the leak

wear tennis shoes   or rubber
soles to climb   there out of sight
where rain turns black

why always at night   or
when a repairman's never around—
regardless   do the job

lightning's brighter than moonlight
to search for cracks
here   no   that's the edge

this storm won't last for forty days
but long enough
to flood the house

better do the job
before slipping again
down   into the damned black water

you don't have nine lives

what is it like
to die
                "a sleep & a forgetting"
as birth is
                waking to remember

is it really
the irrevocable
                lapse of memory
like turning
                blank after blank page
or trying
to read in the dark
                after power fails

is it the nightmare
                without end
the last night
                without dreams
is it today
                without tomorrow

what is it like
                to die

hemlock

these blown blossoms   hippocrates   will not flower again
(now needs not whence . . .
i will not be one more living with decay
wilful seeds planted   nurtured   cultured   grew mature
taking space & time

(the hourglass needs turning . . .
but let this be the last
now i will do it
out of turn
to be out
of time

epilogue

the dog catchers

. . . are out today
are all your cards
papers passports
& dossiers
in order . . . or

will your owner
distraught claim you
. . . or disinterested
let them put you
permanently away

ABOUT THE AUTHOR

Fred Candelaria (2 December 1929), a Canadian citizen since 1973, is originally from El Paso, Texas, where he began university studies before going to Yale and taking his Ph.D. degree at the University of Missouri. Before that he went to St. John's Seminary, where he first studied Latin and bits of Greek. Because he later added a smattering of French and German to his native Spanish, he was drafted and assigned as a translator in Army Intelligence. After serving as Director of Composition at the University of Oregon, he was invited to join the original faculty of Simon Fraser University in Vancouver in 1965.

He began publishing poems while in graduate school, but his first book of poetry did not appear until he came to Canada. He founded the *West Coast Review* in 1966 and edited it until he took early retirement as Professor Emeritus in 1986 to concentrate on writing, composing, and photography.